Undertaking a fostering assessment

A guide to collecting and analysing information for Form F (Fostering) England

Roger Chapman

www.corambaaf.org.uk

Published by

CoramBAAF Adoption and Fostering Academy

41 Brunswick Square

London WC1N 1AZ

www.corambaaf.org.uk

Coram Academy Limited, registered as a company limited by guarantee in England and
Wales number 9697712, part of the Coram group, charity number 312278

© Roger Chapman 2009

Second edition © Roger Chapman 2014

Third edition © Roger Chapman 2016

Originally published by BAAF. New edition in 2016 by CoramBAAF

British Library Cataloguing in Publication Data

A catalogue record for this book is available from the British Library

ISBN 978 1 910039 55 7

Project management by Shaila Shah, Director of Publications, COramBAAF

Designed and typeset by Helen Joubert Design Ltd

Printed in Great Britain by The Lavenham Press

Contents

Appendices

Acknowledgements

I would like to thank Shaila Shah, Colin Bent, Mo O'Reilly and Elaine Dibben from CoramBAAF for their helpful comments, input and encouragement in shaping the first edition, and to Paul Adams from CoramBAAF for his input on the second.

I would also like to thank staff at Northamptonshire County Council and independent fostering providers including Alliance Foster Care, TACT, Fosterplus, Compass, ISP, Fostering Outcomes and Pathway for their positive feedback and the opportunity to "fine tune" this guide while undertaking assessments. I acknowledge that the guide may include elements of good practice I have absorbed from them.

Finally, thanks must go to my wife Jenny for her support, encouragement and patience while I have spent many weekends putting this guide together, and to my sons Tom and James for their invaluable help when my computer would not do what I wanted it to.

The author

Roger Chapman is an independent social worker based in Northamptonshire. He qualified as a social worker in 1980 and began his career in child care in Rochdale.

In 1986 he took up a position in the Fostering Team of Northamptonshire County Council where he remained until 2006. From 2000 he held the position of Team Manager there. During his time in Northamptonshire, he had extensive experience of undertaking assessments of foster carers himself and supervising others engaged in this task. He also spent four years as adviser to the County's fostering panel.

Sine 2006, he has been working independently offering consultancy; undertaking assessments and annual reviews of foster carers; providing training for staff in assessment and sitting as an independent member on fostering panels. Between 2007 and 2011 he was a non-lay member of the GSCC Registration and Conduct Committee and since 2010 he has been a non-lay member of the Independent Review Mechanism (IRM) Panel.

In addition to this guide, Roger has also designed and produced a board game entitled *Welcome to our Family* (available from CoramBAAF) for use with families with birth children to help engage them in the assessment process.

How to use this guide

Introduction

This guide is designed to help social workers conduct a comprehensive assessment of prospective applicants who want to foster a child or children. It is to be used by assessing social workers to complete a **Prospective Foster Carer report (Form F (England))**, published by BAAF in 2014, now available from CoramBAAF.

The guide is primarily based on Section B of Form F, which pulls together information about the applicant – what has made them into the person they are today and what creates the stability and security in their adult life that will have a bearing on their ability to become a foster carer. The information covers the applicant as an individual, their family and wider environmental factors before moving on to consider their capacity to undertake the task of fostering.

It is expected that assessing social workers will be familiar with Form F. However, below is a brief overview of its structure.

A brief overview of the structure of Prospective Foster Carer report Form F (England)

Front sheet

The front sheet provides very basic information about the prospective foster carer(s) and the fostering service. It includes the social work recommendation about their approval and contains a pen picture of the prospective foster carer(s).

Section A – Factual information

Section A records primarily factual information about the applicant and their household. Part 1 reflects the information that is required to be collected under Stage 1 of the assessment process as laid down in the July 2013 Amendments to the Children Act 1989

(Assessment and Approval of Foster Carers). Part 2 includes verification of documents and other checks and factual information, as required for Stage 2 of the assessment process.

Section B – Description and analysis

Section B covers more detailed description and analysis and is set out in three subsections. The first is about the applicant's history, family and lifestyle; the second is an assessment of their fostering capacity; and the third looks at the applicant's preparation for the fostering task. It is Section B that this guide is primarily aimed at.

Section C – Supporting information

This section collates supporting information including material that is legally required (such as personal references) and other documents such as family trees, ecomaps, chronologies and checklists (depending on the policy of the fostering service).

Section D – Specialist reports

Where relevant, the assessor may include additional reports relating to parent and child fostering, permanent fostering, short-break fostering for disabled children, remand fostering or other specialist fostering schemes. Some suggestions for areas to cover when considering recommending applicants for approval for such schemes are included in this guide.

Section E – Summary and recommendation

Section E consists of the summary and recommendation of the assessing social worker and is signed by them and the responsible manager. It also includes the applicant's observations on the report.

Additional tools and resources

Some tools and resources are provided to help the assessor with collecting and presenting some of the information required for this report. Additionally, there are tools that the fostering service might utilise as part of the assessment process.

What this guide is

This guide primarily takes Section B of the CoramBAAF Form F and breaks down each area into three parts for exploration with the applicant:

- a list of questions that can be asked of the applicant or can be used to facilitate further discussion in order to collect some of the basic information required for the purposes of the assessment;

- some suggestions for how the information that has been collected can be analysed to see if it may provide evidence that may be positive for fostering or could be seen as a potential area of concern or vulnerability by the assessing social worker (referred to as the "assessor");

- for some of the areas covered, how the information given could be verified from sources both within and outside of the family.

Where appropriate, relevant sections from the guidance notes that accompany the CoramBAAF Form F have also been included before the suggested list of questions for that area.

It is hoped that, by making use of this guide, the assessor will be able to collect the information that will form the basis of a sound assessment.

Having collected the information, the guide places an emphasis on the **analysis** of the information collected and there is a designated space for this analysis to be presented in Form F after each area covered in Section B. It is important to ensure that the analysis section does contain a detailed examination and interpretation of the information collected and is not a re-stating of that, or new, information.

It is also intended that the guide may help the assessor in the planning of sessions with their supervisor and with the applicant themselves. There is a helpful timesheet in Appendix 2 that can be used, in conjunction with CoramBAAF's Assessment Agreement, to plan out the course of the assessment and agree in what order areas will be covered and within what timescale. Personal style may dictate in what order the areas are covered but some thought should be given to this as it may be more appropriate to cover the more personal, and perhaps painful, areas of people's lives once a relationship has been established between the assessor and the applicant.

The information in the appendices is intended to complement each agency's own procedures and formats for these areas. These include the following.

- An example of how to present an ecomap detailing where the applicant gets their support from and an example of a family tree.

- The aforementioned timesheet to assist in the overall planning of the assessment.

- A plan for an interview with a personal referee for the applicant.

- Suggestions of areas to cover in a health and safety check of the applicant's home.

- Suggestions of areas to be covered in a family safer caring policy.

What this guide is not

This guide is not intended to be a quick and easy way of undertaking an assessment. It offers a way of collecting the basic information needed to complete the process. Although most of the guide is presented in question format, it is not intended that the questions merely be fired at the applicant. Rather, they are designed to help the assessor cover key areas in what should be a dynamic process rather than one that consists merely of answers to questions or the completion of a checklist.

The assessor must be alert to the idiosyncrasies and complexities of each applicant they assess and be prepared to pursue different lines of questioning and exploration accordingly and analyse that information on the basis of its relevance to the fostering task.

Nor should the guide lead to any standardisation of assessments. It is important for assessors to maintain their individual styles of seeking, analysing and presenting information.

The guide should be seen as a tool to help in the assessment process and not an end in itself.

Family background and childhood (including education)

The assessor should pay attention during these interviews not only to the information provided by the applicant but to the quality of the response. This should enable the assessor to come to a view of the extent to which the applicant has resolved past traumas or losses; has the capacity to make and sustain close relationships; and is able to empathise and understand other people's feelings and be able to reflect on emotive matters.

- Compile a family tree (include dates of birth and whether family members are living or deceased. This could be completed by the applicant prior to this session or jointly with them and should be included in Section C of the Form F. Bear in mind that when completing the exercise of compiling a family tree, many of the issues listed below will be covered).

- Where were you born and raised?

- Describe your mother and the nature of your relationship with her.

- Describe your father and the nature of your relationship with him.

- What employment were your parents engaged in?

- Give details of any other significant caregivers or adults in your childhood.

- As a child, to whom did you feel closest and why?

- Describe your relationship with your siblings.

- What good things do you remember about your childhood?

- What unhappy memories or times do you remember?

- Which schools did you attend?

- What are your memories and experiences of primary and junior school?

- How would you describe your overall experience of early childhood (i.e. pre-adolescence)?

- What are your significant memories of your teenage years?

- What was your experience of secondary school?

- What was the attitude of your parents towards your education?

- Did you gain any qualifications from school and, if so, which?

- Was adolescence a time of experimentation for you?

- What was your overall experience of adolescence?

- What are your memories of special occasions (birthdays, religious or cultural festivals, holidays)?

- What was your overall experience of being parented?

- How do you feel your experiences as a child have shaped the person you are today?

ANALYSIS

- **What experiences from their background and experience of childhood can the applicant bring to fostering (e.g. experience of loss, separation, feeling different, poor parenting or benefits from a happy, stable background)?**

- **What is the applicant's experience of attachment to parents/caregivers?**

- **Where this has been poor, what evidence is there that they have been able to overcome this?**

- **Is the applicant able to be reflective about their experiences?**

Verify through:

- **Personal and family member references**

Adult life (including employment and previous relationships)

This information is important in getting a sense of the applicant and their life experience and, in many ways, this section is a continuation of the applicant's life history. The information will be important in conveying how the applicant's past has made them into the person they have become, providing information about whether they have achieved stability in their lives, how they might manage stresses and difficulties,

and what they have learned about themselves that will be relevant in relation to fostering children and young people.

Education/employment

- Have you had any experience of further or higher education?
- Have you gained any qualifications or skills as an adult?
- How would you assess your computer and literacy skills, taking account of the requirement of foster carers to maintain a level and standard of record keeping?
- Will you need any help or support to meet this requirement?
- What is your attitude to education now as a parent/potential foster carer?
- Give details of your experience of work from leaving school to the present day (pay particular attention to work involving children or caring) and explain any gaps in your employment history.
- Have you had experience of working as a member of a team?
- What opportunities have you had for training in your employment?
- How have you benefited from these?
- How important is work to you?
- What are your ambitions/plans for the future with regard to working?
- How will your work commitments fit around fostering? Have you discussed this with your employer?

Previous relationships

- Have you had any previous significant relationships?
- Who was the relationship with?
- How long did it last and when did it start and finish?
- What was the status of the relationship?
- Why did the relationship end?
- Were there children in or from the relationship?
- With whom did they live after the relationship ended and how was this decided?
- How were the children affected by the break-up?
- How did you help them deal with this?
- What contact is there now with your ex-partner and any children?
- If contact for the children is, or was involved, how has this been managed?
- If children from a previous relationship visit or stay over, how often does this happen, what does this involve and where do the children sleep?
- What is the attitude of these children to this fostering application?

- How will their needs be met, alongside those of the foster children, when they visit?

- What impact might these relationships have on fostering?

- What have you learnt from your previous relationship/s?

- Can we contact the ex-partner/s for a reference?

- If not, what are the reasons for this?

- If this is not possible, are there referees who knew you when you were in that relationship who could be contacted?

Adult life

- What have been the significant events in your adult life?

- What has been your experience of religion in your life?

- How do you see your culture and how is this reflected in your upbringing and life now?

- What efforts do you make to try to maintain a good level of health?

- Do you now, or have you in the past, suffered from any significant illnesses, including any mental health difficulties?

- If so, would these affect in any way your ability to care for a child?

- What is your attitude to smoking and alcohol use?

- Do you feel you are a strong person emotionally?

- How have you managed and responded to any stressful episodes in your life?

- What has given you the greatest satisfaction in your life so far?

- What has been the biggest disappointment for you?

ANALYSIS

- **What is your assessment of the applicant's ability to undertake the level of record keeping required of a foster carer?**

- **Are there any areas in which the agency might need to offer support or training in record keeping?**

- **How will the applicant manage liaising with schools about the child's education and will they attend parents' evenings?**

- **Are there skills or experiences from the applicant's work experience that would be transferable to fostering?**

- **Has the applicant demonstrated a positive attitude towards training and personal development?**

- **How flexible is the applicant in terms of fitting work around fostering?**

- What is your assessment of the applicant's ability to cover child care during school holidays or periods of exclusion or if a child is ill?

- Is there corroboration of the details of any previous relationship from the ex-partner or a referee who knew them when they were together?

- If there are children from a previous relationship, what is the evidence that their needs have been fully considered in this application?

- Can any experience of arranging contact for their own children be helpful in terms of thinking about contact for foster children?

- What evidence is there that the current relationship is more likely to succeed than the previous one (if applicable)?

- Are there any issues arising from any other significant relationships the applicant has had that might have a bearing on this application?

- What is your assessment of the effect on fostering of any physical or mental health issues that have been raised by the applicant?

- Does the applicant appear emotionally robust enough to foster?

- What evidence is there of their resilience and ability to deal with difficulties?

- What evidence is there of insight into how the applicant's past has shaped them as adults today?

- What are the contra-indications or potential areas of vulnerability from their adult life and how could these risks be minimised or gaps filled?

Verify through:

- Personal and family member references
- Ex-partner references
- Employer references
- Interviews with other children of the applicants
- Medical reports

Personality and current relationship

The assessor will be able to make judgements about the applicant's personality based on their self-reporting, views of their partner if they have one, views of birth children and from the range of other references and information available. It will be important to check that there is a consistent picture emerging from all these sources. The assessment of the stability and permanence of a couple's relationship should include

the history of that relationship, how well it works and the couple's commitment to it. It should explore what has tested the relationship and how the partners support each other.

- How would you describe yourself?

- Do you share any characteristics with your parents?

- How would you assess your own strengths and weaknesses?

- What evidence can you give that shows you are organised, reliable and dependable?

- How would others describe you, including your partner (if applicable)?

- If you have a partner, do you have any similar or complementary qualities to them?

- How, where and when did you meet your current partner?

- How did the relationship develop?

- What do you feel makes the relationship successful?

- What qualities do each of you bring to the relationship?

- How much time do you spend together?

- What roles do each of you have in the relationship?

- How do you make decisions?

- How do you deal with problems, disagreements, stress and anger both individually and as a couple?

- What issues can cause these?

- How do you celebrate success?

- How do you manage failure or disappointment?

- How do you support each other?

- How do you show affection?

- What do you see as the strengths of the relationship?

- What are the vulnerable areas?

- How do you think fostering might affect your relationship?

- (If applicant is single) Are you looking for a relationship or, if one develops, how would you manage this if you were fostering?

- (If the applicants are in a gay or lesbian partnership) How would you discuss your relationship with any children placed with you?

ANALYSIS

- **What personal qualities does the applicant have that may be positive for fostering?**

- **Are there any concerns about the applicant's personality?**

- What evidence is there that the applicant's current relationship is a secure and stable one?
- Is there evidence to suggest that this relationship is strong enough to deal with the stresses and strains that fostering can bring?
- Is there evidence of mutual support?
- Could a foster child exploit any areas of vulnerability in the relationship?

Verify through:

- Personal and family member references
- Relevant relationship documentation

Household members (including children) and lifestyle

The assessor should provide a brief pen picture of each household member and each one should be interviewed. Information from those interviews can be included here but if the household member wishes this to be confidential, it should be included in Section C. Research suggests that where birth children are consulted, listened to, involved and prepared, then they are likely to be better placed to support their parent's fostering.

- Give details of any children in the family.
- What is the relationship of the children to the applicant?
- Describe the personality and character of each child.
- What are their interests and talents?
- How are they managing at nursery/school/college?
- What is their understanding of fostering?
- Do they know any children who are looked after/fostered?
- How did you raise the issue of fostering with them?
- How involved have they been in the application process?
- Have you taken account of their views?
- What do you think will be the benefits of fostering for them?
- What are the areas in which they might be vulnerable?
- What has been their experience of sharing your time/their possessions?

- What is the nature of their relationship with their siblings (if applicable)?

- Do any special relationships exist between the children and the applicant?

NB. If the applicant has grandchildren who visit or stay, adapt the above questions accordingly and consider whether it would be useful to interview them.

Interviews with a child/children

The interviews with the children themselves will be planned according to their age and level of understanding, but could include the following:

- How was the idea of fostering raised with you?

- What was your reaction?

- Have you been kept involved in the process?

- Do you know any children who are fostered or looked after?

- Why do you think children may need foster families?

- How do you think fostering might affect you?

- How could you help foster children to settle into your family and neighbourhood?

- What are the good things about living in your family?

- How prepared are you to share with foster children (toys, parents, etc)?

- What sex and age of child do you think will fit best into your family and why?

- What would you do if you were upset or unhappy about something to do with fostering?

- Are there people outside of your family to whom you would talk if you were unhappy?

- Are there any things that worry you about fostering?

- What do you think will be the rewards of fostering for you and your family and what might be difficult?

ANALYSIS

(If the applicant has grandchildren, then consider the issues raised below in relation to them.)

- **How well has the applicant prepared and involved their children for the task of fostering?**

- **Does the applicant have insight into the possible effects (positive and negative) of fostering on their own children?**

- **Has the applicant taken into account the needs of their own children when considering the type of fostering they want to do and the age group/sex of foster children they wish to be considered for?**

- **How resilient do the children appear to be?**

- **How realistic do the children appear to be about the task of fostering?**

- **Are there areas where the children may be vulnerable and, if so, what action could be taken to minimise this?**

- **Is there evidence that their own children have an outlet for expressing any concerns or worries about fostering?**

Other adults in the household

- Are there other adult members of your household?

- What is their relationship to you?

- How would you describe them as individuals?

- What work do they do?

- What experience of children do they have?

- How much time do they spend in the home?

- How do they feel about fostering?

- What are the implications for them if you foster?

- Have you considered what information you will and will not share with these individuals about the children you might foster?

- How will you ensure that both they, and the children you might foster, will remain safe?

- What role are they likely to play in respect of fostering either by offering direct care of the child or more general support?

- Do they have any particular experience, skills or interests that could benefit your fostering?

ANALYSIS

- **From your interviews with these adults, what is your impression of their attitude towards fostering?**

- **Is there evidence that these people could play a positive role in fostering?**

- **Could they be vulnerable in any way and, if so, what action could be taken to minimise this?**

- **Has the applicant grasped the importance of confidentiality but balanced this against the need to keep other adult members of the household safe?**

> **Verify through:**
>
> - Interviews with birth children and other members of the household
>
> - Personal and family member references
>
> - DBS disclosures on other adults in the household

Lifestyle

In providing information about lifestyle and leisure, the assessor has the opportunity to give a good picture of the family in day-to-day life and consider how a foster child might experience living in the home.

- Describe a typical weekend for your household.

- Describe the routine during the week.

- Who does what in the family and are gender roles important?

- What are the written or unwritten "rules" that exist in the family?

- What is your attitude to food (healthy *vs* convenient/fast food)?

- What leisure activities do family members enjoy individually and as a family?

- Do you have a computer and access to the internet?

- What role do religious/cultural practices play in your household?

- How do you celebrate special occasions (birthdays/religious and cultural festivals/anniversaries)?

- What kind of holidays do you enjoy?

- How is affection displayed in your family?

- How do you deal with people's feelings in your family? Do family members pick up on how others are feeling? Do you encourage discussion? Can you think of any examples?

- Who else visits the family home on a regular basis and what role would they have with a foster child placed?

ANALYSIS

- **What evidence is there that there is space in this family's lifestyle to accommodate foster children?**

- **How flexible or rigid are they with regard to routines?**

- **How comfortable would a foster child feel in becoming a part of this family and is there anything that might make this difficult?**

- **What evidence is there that this is a family that deals with feelings and emotions?**

Verify through:

- **Personal and family member references**
- **Interviews with children or other adults in the family**

Other children (including adults) and social support network

This section should include information about all other children (including adult children) who are not living in the household. The assessor should provide a pen picture for each, provide information about their relationship with the applicant and consider how fostering might impact on them and their relationship with the applicant. Children living outside of the home should normally be interviewed as part of the assessment. When considering the support network, the assessor is required to set out the supportive relationships that already exist within the applicant's network and provide information about the type and quality of support they might be able to access in a fostering context.

- Do you have other children, including those who are adults, living elsewhere?

- Can you tell us about them (i.e. where they live, what they do, their personality, etc)?

- How often do you have contact with them and when?

- What are their feelings about you fostering?

- Are there any implications for them if you foster?

- Have you considered what information you will and will not share with these individuals about the child you might foster?

- How will you ensure that both they, and the child you might foster, will remain safe when they are with you?

- What role are they likely to play in respect of fostering either by offering direct care of the child or more general support?

- Do they have any particular experience, skills or interests that could benefit your fostering?

- Do they have any children of their own?

- If so, what would be the nature of their involvement with any child you might foster?

- Can you tell us about any other people you see on a regular or frequent basis who will have contact with any foster child?

ANALYSIS

- **Which of these people discussed above have been interviewed as part of this assessment?**

- **Is there evidence that these people could play a positive role in fostering?**

- **Could they be vulnerable in any way and, if so, what action could be taken to minimise this?**

> **Verify through:**
>
> - **Interviews with adult children living elsewhere**

Social support network

- Complete a support network ecomap (an example of an ecomap can be found in Appendix 1). Include the following for each entry:

  - Name

  - Relationship to applicant

  - Ethnicity

  - Faith

  - Where they live

  - Frequency of contact

  - Nature of support offered now

  - What role they might play with foster children (and whether they have skills or experience that could be of benefit)

  - Age of own children and what role they might play

  - Also include details of any groups/clubs to which the applicant belongs and that provide support

- Would any of these people be very involved in the care of any foster child (do they need a DBS check)?

- For single applicants, what would happen if you were unable to care for the foster child for any reason?

- To whom do you feel closest and why (If this is your partner, who would be next outside of that relationship)?

- Can you recall a recent stressful incident/issue? Who did you confide in and why? How was the matter resolved?

- Do you share all problems with others or do you deal with some on your own?

- What is your understanding of "confidentiality" and how do you practise this amongst family, friends and neighbours?

- Why do you think maintaining confidentiality is important when fostering?

- How would you ensure that a foster child remains safe from physical and sexual abuse in your network of family, friends and acquaintances and that they, in turn, remain safe from allegations?

- What support do you expect to receive while fostering?

- How would you set about establishing a positive working relationship with your Supervising Social Worker?

- Are you aware of the importance of practising safer caring and what might happen if an allegation is made against you?

- Can you think of how or why an allegation might be made against you?

- Are you aware of national organisations, such as Fostering Network and Coram BAAF, that can offer independent, external advice and support?

- Are you aware that you can make complaints or compliments on behalf of yourself or any children you are fostering regarding the service you receive?

ANALYSIS

- **How accessible is the support network?**

- **How robust is the support network?**

- **Does the network contain a range of skills and experience that could be called upon?**

- **Does the applicant understand the importance of confidentiality?**

- **Are there people from different backgrounds, ethnicities/religions, etc, in the support network who could play a positive role in fostering?**

- **If there are gaps in the support network, how could these be filled?**

- **How realistic are the applicant's expectations of support whilst fostering?**

> **Verify through:**
>
> - **Personal and family member references**
> - **Interviews with key people in the support network (if not referees)**
> - **Additional written references, if appropriate**

3

Assessment of fostering capacity

Caring for children: providing warmth, empathy and encouragement

In this section, the assessor is asked to provide information about the applicant's experience and abilities in relation to caring for children, with evidence being provided about the quality of those relationships in terms of warmth, empathy and commitment. This may relate to birth children, children of friends or relatives, or children who have been known in professional or other work capacities. It is important to be aware that Sinclair *et al* (2005) identified positive outcomes for foster carers who were caring, encouraging and able to see things from a child's perspective.

- What does being a parent mean to you?

- How did you adjust to becoming a parent?

- Thinking of your own experience of being parented, what have you changed and what have you kept the same in being a parent yourself?

- What experience do you have of children, both your own and those of other people?

- What have been the rewards and the challenges for you of being a parent?

- How do you think a foster child might be feeling about coming to live with you?

- How would you make a foster child feel welcome in your home?

- How would you try to make sure a foster child was happy living with you?

- How do you/would you demonstrate warmth and affection towards children?

- Can you think of different ways in which you might communicate with children?

- How can you help build a child's self-confidence and self-esteem?

- How could you encourage children to achieve their potential in education or other activities they try?

- Can you think of examples of how you have treated children as individuals?

- How can you help children and young people to make decisions and learn from any mistakes they make?

- Can you think of any times when you have helped children and young people cope with big changes in their lives and how you achieved this?

- How can you help children and young people maintain a good standard of physical and emotional health?

ANALYSIS

- **Is there evidence that the applicant has been successful in parenting their own children? How might this transfer to fostering?**

- **What do you see as the applicant's strengths as a parent?**

- **Do you have any concerns about their parenting?**

- **What experience have they had with other people's children and what have they learnt from this that they could bring to fostering?**

- **Is there evidence that the applicant would promote life opportunities for foster children?**

- **How do you feel a foster child would experience this family?**

- **What evidence is there that the applicant can provide a warm and caring environment for a foster child?**

- **What evidence is there of the applicant's capacity to empathise?**

Verify through:

- **Personal and family member references**

- **Interviews with applicant's birth or step-children**

- **Education references**

- **References from previous employers where work has involved children**

- **Feedback from pre-approval training course**

- **Using case studies as exercises**

Caring for children: providing structure and boundaries

This section asks about the ability of the applicant to provide clear structure and boundaries for children in their care. Research evidence

(Quinton *et al*, 1998; Sinclair *et al*, 2005) suggests that successful outcomes are most likely where foster carers are able to offer routine and structure, have clear expectations, set boundaries and manage behaviour. This also requires sensitivity, emotional robustness and a focus on the reinforcement of positive behaviour.

- What is your understanding and experience of child development and attachment?

- Do you understand how children can become stuck at different stages of their development?

- How do you manage children's behaviour?

- How would you try to manage the behaviour of a child who was acting in a way that suggested they were younger or older than their chronological age?

- What strategies might you use to manage the behaviour of children in the age group that you would like to foster?

- What are your views on the use of corporal punishment?

- How would you encourage positive behaviour?

- How would you reward children?

- How would you ensure the safety of the children of the age group you would like to foster, both inside and outside of your home?

- How would you balance safety with encouraging some independence?

- If a child wanted to do something you considered to be risky or dangerous, how would you deal with this?

- What boundaries do you feel are important with teenagers?

- What techniques would you employ for discussions or negotiations with teenagers?

- Have you had experience of discussing issues such as drugs, alcohol and sexual health with children and young people?

- How might you approach these issues with foster children?

- How do you/would you manage the use of the internet and other social media with children and young people?

- What is your understanding and awareness of the risks to children of sexual exploitation?

- What do you see as the role of parents and foster carers with regard to fulfilling educational requirements?

ANALYSIS

- **Do you think the applicant's understanding of child development and attachment is sufficient to begin fostering?**

- **Does the applicant manage the behaviour of children in an appropriate way?**

- Does the applicant have a range of different strategies that they could employ?
- Would they benefit from training or support in this area?
- What is the evidence that they can keep children safe?
- How realistic is the applicant about managing the challenges that teenagers can present?
- How do you assess the applicant's understanding and awareness of the potential risks to children and young people from use of social media and from sexual exploitation?
- Would they benefit from further training or support in this area?

Verify through:

- Personal and family member references
- Interviews with birth children
- Feedback from pre-approval training course
- The family's safer caring plan
- Using case studies as exercises

Caring for children: providing durability, resilience and commitment

A successful foster carer will need to be durable and resilient if they are going to be able to provide a placement for the length of time that is required and to avoid unnecessary placement moves for children. Children and young people are clear that they want foster carers who will "stick with them", advocate for them and show a commitment over and above what is required in legislation (Sinclair *et al*, 2005).

- How do you manage stress in your life?
- Can you think of any stressful or difficult times you have experienced and say how you dealt with these?
- Can you describe any experiences you have had of managing children or adults with challenging behaviour?
- Is there evidence from other areas of your life in which you have demonstrated the resilience or determination to see things through to their conclusion?
- What do you think might be some of the challenges you could face as a foster carer?

- How prepared do you feel to manage these?

- How, when and where would you seek help if you were experiencing difficulties?

- Are there any types of behaviour that you would feel unable to manage and, if so, why?

- Can you think of how you could show a foster child that you were committed to caring for them?

- What do you think might be the effect on a foster child of having to move between different families in different areas?

- As a foster carer, how could you show the child that you want to offer them stability and security?

- How do you think you would measure your success as a foster carer?

ANALYSIS

- **Has the applicant evidenced the ability or potential to manage stress and challenges?**

- **How realistic is the applicant about the challenges they might face as a foster carer?**

- **What help and support might the applicant need to sustain the placements of children and will they ask for it?**

- **Can the applicant demonstrate any evidence of resilience and commitment?**

Verify through:

- **Personal and family member references**

- **Case studies as exercises**

- **Feedback from pre-approval training course**

Working effectively with others

Systems theory helps us to understand that the success of a placement will often depend on how well the different parties can work together in the best interests of the child. Foster carers are expected to work closely with other members of the fostering team, social workers, birth parents, schools and others. In assessing suitability against this particular quality, the assessor will need to use the information gathered throughout the assessment, taking account of the various references and checks that

have been undertaken that relate to both their professional and private life. The assessment will need to consider specifically the applicant's capacity for working with the child's birth family and promoting contact.

- What do you think are some of the benefits of working as part of a team?

- Can you think of times in your life where you have worked as part of a team?

- What qualities or skills do you think you can bring to a team?

- What do you think can help to make teams work successfully and what can prevent this from happening?

- As a parent, which other professionals have you worked with and what was the nature of your working relationship with them?

- As a foster carer, who do you think are the other people and professionals you might be working alongside for the benefit of the child?

- As a foster carer, how would you try to maximise your contribution to this group and help it to work as effectively as possible?

- Can you see any difficulty in working as a part of this group and at the same time acting as an advocate for the child? If so, how would you manage this?

- Why do you think parents have the difficulties that they do in caring for their children?

- Have you had any involvement with contact arrangements as a child or a parent, for example, as a result of family break-up?

- Why is it important for children to maintain contact with members of their own family or people who are important to them?

- How could you help make this as positive an experience as possible for the child?

- Are you aware of the restrictions and commitments that contact arrangements may have on you and your family?

- What are the different ways in which contact could be maintained?

- How do you think a child might feel before and after a meeting with members of their family?

- How might a foster child living with you feel at times like birthdays and Christmas or other festivals?

- How would you promote the child's family for them in between periods of contact?

- Would you be prepared to meet with the parents or other family members of the child?

- How do you think they might feel meeting you and knowing their child is in foster care?

- If the parents became aggressive or threatening, what would you do?

- Can you think of what information you might share with parents and what you would not?

- If the Care Plan for the child is to return to their own home, how could you work with their family to help make this happen?

- Are there any restrictions you would place on working with the child's family?

ANALYSIS

- **Is there evidence that the applicant can, or has the potential to, work effectively as a member of a team?**

- **Does the applicant have a realistic understanding of their role as a foster carer in working alongside others?**

- **Does the applicant demonstrate an understanding of why children need foster care and can they empathise with parents in any way?**

- **Do you think the applicant could work positively with parents?**

- **Have they had any personal experience of contact that might be relevant to fostering?**

- **Do they demonstrate an understanding of how contact might affect children?**

- **Do they understand the value of maintaining contact?**

- **Will the demands of contact fit into the applicant's lifestyle?**

- **Are there any gaps in the applicant's understanding or areas where they might be vulnerable in working with members of the child's family?**

Verify through:

- **Employment references**

- **Education references**

- **Personal references**

- **Reference from ex-partner**

- **Interviews with children from any previous relationships**

- **Feedback from pre-approval training course**

Understanding identity and diversity

The statutory guidance on fostering services issued in 2013 requires that 'every individual child who is looked after should be cared for in a way that respects, recognises, supports and celebrates their identity' and that foster carers 'should ensure that full attention is paid to the child's gender, faith, ethnic origin, cultural and linguistic background, sexual orientation and any disability they might have'. However, it is important to recognise that not all applicants will have a sophisticated understanding of all the issues at the time they are being assessed as foster carers; what is most important is that they have the appropriate value base and willingness to learn if their understanding is limited.

- What do you understand the term "identity" to mean?

- What do you think are some of the component parts that make up your own sense of identity or describe who you are?

- How would you describe your own identity in terms of your gender, ethnicity, disability, class, culture, language, sexuality and spirituality?

- Which groups of people do you feel you belong to and what sets you aside as more of an individual?

- Do you know where your name originates from or why it was chosen for you?

- What do you know of your family history?

- Why is it important to care for a child in a way that maintains a positive sense of their own identity?

- How would you nurture the identity of a foster child you were caring for?

- How do you view Britain today in terms of the mix of different racial and cultural groups that exist?

- What is the ethnic mix of your own local area?

- Does your lifestyle reflect the fact that we live in a multiracial/multicultural society (i.e. food, music, friends, interests, etc)?

- Have you ever experienced any prejudice or bullying?

- Can you give some examples of reasons people might be discriminated against in society?

- What steps would you take if you felt a foster child was a victim of prejudice, bullying or discrimination of any kind?

- What contact do you have, or have had, with people of different ethnicities, people with a learning or physical disability or those of a sexuality different to your own?

- Do you have any people in your social and support network who could offer you any help with caring for a child of a different ethnicity, faith, or sexuality to your own or with a child who has a physical or learning disability?

- How did your parents and extended family relate to people from different racial and religious backgrounds or people who were disabled or gay or lesbian?

- How has this affected your own attitudes and values and how have you raised your own children in relation to these issues? Give examples of how you have discussed these matters with them (there may be examples of issues raised on TV or by friends and people in your network or situations they have experienced at school).

- If you were asked to care for a child from a different racial/cultural/religious background to your own, how would you feel and what would you do?

- How would you communicate with a child whose language was different to your own?

- If you were asked to care for a child with a physical or learning disability, how would you feel and what would you do?

- If you were asked to care for a young person who was gay, lesbian or uncertain of their sexuality, how would you feel and what would you do?

- Do you understand that foster children may come from backgrounds where their own families hold and express discriminatory views and they may have absorbed some or all of these attitudes and values?

- How would you help a child develop a positive view of Britain as a multiracial/ multicultural society?

ANALYSIS

- **How well do you feel the applicant understands the concept of identity and its importance? What additional help and support might help the applicant to develop this awareness further?**

- **Is there evidence that the applicant has non-discriminatory attitudes and values that are consistent with learning in this area?**

- **Has the applicant had any personal experience that might help them care for a child from a different ethnicity, sexuality or with a physical or learning disability?**

- **Are there people in their family and friends network who could help the applicant care for a child with a disability or from a different ethnicity, faith or sexuality to that of their own?**

- **Where there are family members of the applicant with discriminatory attitudes, has the applicant given thought to how they would deal with this and is the assessor satisfied that this will not expose children to negative experiences?**

- **Does the assessor feel confident that this is a family who would challenge prejudice and bullying in an appropriate way if it arose?**

- **How comfortable would a child from a different ethnicity, faith, sexuality or with a disability feel living in this family and in the local area?**

- **Are there areas in which the applicant might benefit from further training?**

Verify through:

- **Personal and family member references**

- **Feedback from pre-approval training course**

- **Case studies as exercises**

- **Ecomap (evidence of potential support to applicants)**

Preparing to foster

4

Motivation and timing of application

It is helpful, when considering the applicant's suitability, to understand their motivation for fostering and what they want to get out of it. The assessor will need to be clear about why the applicant has applied at this particular time, how this has been considered in relation to all household members, and how realistic this is.

- How long have you been thinking about fostering?

- What was the starting point?

- Why is now the right time for you to proceed?

- Are there other reasons why you would like to foster?

- How is the timing of this application right for other household members?

- Why do you feel you would make a good foster carer?

- What type of fostering do you feel would be best for your family and why?

- What age group of children do you feel you might be best suited to and why?

- What are you hoping fostering will give you?

- Do you know any other foster carers or fostered children?

- How did you find out about this fostering agency and why did you choose this one?

ANALYSIS

- **Does the applicant's motivation to foster seem genuine and realistic and is it based on meeting the needs of the child?**

- **Does the timing of this application seem right for all members of the household?**

- **How important is the financial element of fostering to the applicant?**

> **Verify through:**
>
> - **Personal and family member references**
> - **Interviews with other members of the household**
> - **Reference from previous fostering agency (if transferring)**

Childlessness or limitation of family size

In cases where childlessness or limitation of family size is a motivating factor for fostering, the assessor may wish to consider the following areas with the applicant.

Childless applicants

- What is the reason for not having, or being able to have, children of your own?
- How and when was this discovered?
- At the time, how did you react to and deal with this?
- How did you support each other?
- What efforts have you made to explore alternative methods of having your own family and over what period of time?
- When did these efforts cease?
- How have you adjusted to the outcome?
- Do you still take any precautions to prevent a possible pregnancy?
- Why do you feel now is the right time to consider fostering?
- Are you aware that some feelings around infertility may arise again in the future at different times?
- How might you feel if a foster child you have become attached to moves on from you in the future?

Applicants with children

- Has the number of children you have had been limited in any way and, if so, why and how have you coped with this?
- Did you plan to have a certain number of children?
- Do you plan to have more children of your own in the future and if so, when and how many?
- How will fostering fit in with these plans?

● Are you currently taking precautions to prevent a pregnancy?

ANALYSIS

● **Is there evidence that the applicant has come to terms with any issues of loss?**

● **Have they moved on to be ready to foster other people's children?**

● **If the applicant plans to have more children of their own, how realistic is this in respect of their fostering application?**

Verify through:

• **Medical references**

• **Personal and family member references**

Preparation, training and expectations

At the start of this section, the assessor should include information about the overall preparation of the applicants and include details of the pre-approval training they have attended if this is not being included in Section C. The assessor should also include feedback on the applicants from the pre-approval training course leaders, again if this is not being included in Section C.

● How would you describe the overall preparation the agency has provided for you in respect of your application to foster?

● How useful did you find the pre-approval training course and what were your main learning points from this?

● How do you respond to the feedback from the training course leaders?

● Are there any particular areas you feel you need to learn more about?

● What do you think might be the differences between being a parent and being a foster carer?

● Do you have any knowledge or experience of children who are looked after?

● How might you expect a child to react to being separated from their parents or carers?

● How might you expect a child who has been abused in the past to behave in your home?

- If a foster child started to tell you about abuse that had occurred in the past, what would you do?

- If foster children have not had a good experience of attachment to their parents or previous caregivers, how might this affect them and their behaviour?

- Can you understand how some foster children are "stuck" in their development and may act younger than their actual age?

- How might foster carers be able to help such children?

- How might you communicate with very young children or those who function below their chronological age?

- How would you help a foster child to attend school, join in play and activities and make friends?

- How would you help a foster child who had no school place or who had been excluded from school?

- How would you help a foster child build up their self-esteem and make them more resilient?

- How would you manage the differing needs if you had more than one foster child?

- How would you ensure that the needs of your own children were also met?

- Might there be any conflict between the way you manage the behaviour of your own children and that of foster children?

- Do you understand that, for some children who have been abused, punishments such as sending them to their room may not be appropriate?

- Why do you think it is important, as a foster carer, to keep clear, concise and factual records?

- How might those records be needed in the future?

- In what other ways can you help the child preserve their memories of their stay with you?

- What do you understand by the term "whistleblowing" and what relevance might this have for foster carers?

ANALYSIS

- **Do you feel that the applicant has been sufficiently prepared for fostering?**

- **How realistic is the applicant about the fostering task?**

- **How much preparation or research have they undertaken?**

- **Do they have the potential to make a positive difference to a foster child?**

> **Verify through:**
> * Feedback from pre-approval training course leaders
> * Evidence of reading any books/articles about fostering
> * Personal and family member references
> * Reference from any previous fostering agency

Anticipated impact of fostering

In this section, the assessor should be thinking (with the applicant) about how fostering might impact on the applicant's current lifestyle; what might need to change and how any changes would need to be managed. It is about trying to make sure the applicant is as prepared as they can be for what is generally recognised to be a significant challenge.

* What contact or discussions have you had with people who are fostering and what have you learnt from them about the potential impact of fostering?
* In what ways would fostering fit into your day-to day lifestyle and routines and what would you need to change?
* Would you anticipate any changes to special occasions such as Christmas or other religious festivals, birthdays or holidays if you were fostering?
* How will fostering affect your household financially?
* How will fostering impact on the lifestyle of individual family and household members?
* If you have children at home, how will you be able to meet their needs alongside those of any foster children?
* What is your understanding of the commitments involved with contact, other meetings for foster children, and training and supervision?
* How will you be able to make space for these alongside your other commitments?

ANALYSIS

* **What changes do you feel the applicant may have to make to their lifestyle to accommodate fostering?**
* **How realistic are they being in terms of the time commitment necessary for fostering?**
* **Are you confident that the applicant can manage the number of children and the type of fostering for which they are being recommended?**

> **Verify through:**
> - **Personal and family member references**
> - **Interviews with members of the family or household**
> - **Completing a calendar exercise (i.e. noting current routines and commitments on a calendar and adding commitments relating to fostering)**

Understanding of safer caring

During the assessment, particular consideration needs to be given to whether the applicant has a good understanding of safer caring issues and whether they can apply this understanding in practice to minimise the risk of any allegations being made against them or members of their household. Applicants would do well to undertake some reading on this subject (such as Slade, 2012).

- Do you understand how and why allegations can be made by children about foster carers?

- What does the idea of safer caring mean to you?

- What did you learn about safer caring from your pre-approval training course?

- Have you read any books or articles about safer caring?

- What are the important principles on which to build a safer caring plan?

- How did you prepare the safer caring plan for your family and who was involved in this?

- How have you prepared yourself and any other members of your household to adopt a safer caring approach?

- What are the areas in which you feel you and your family will need to change your current way of doing things to accommodate a safer caring approach?

- How will you prepare members of your extended family and regular visitors to your home to adopt a safer caring approach?

- On what basis will you share information about the foster child with members of your household or extended family and friends network?

ANALYSIS

- **How well has the applicant understood the idea of safer caring?**

- How realistic and effective do you feel their approach to safer caring will be?

- Are you satisfied that the whole family has taken on board the importance of safer caring?

- Are there any vulnerable areas for the supervising social worker to monitor?

- Does the applicant have a good understanding of confidentiality and know when, and with whom, to share information about a child?

Verify through:

- **Personal and family member references**

- **Interviews with members of the household**

- **Evidence of a safer caring plan for the family**

Future training and development

In this section, the assessor is asked to indicate any areas for future training or development that have been identified in the course of the assessment, and this information can be provided in this section and/or in Section C.

- Are there any areas about being a foster carer that you would like to learn more about?

- What method of learning works best for you (i.e. group courses, online training, personal research, etc)?

- Will you need any support to access any of these different kinds of training?

- What is your understanding of the Training, Support and Development Standards for Foster Carers?

ANALYSIS

- **If there are gaps in the applicant's knowledge and experience, show how these could be filled.**

- **Are there any particular priority areas for learning or development?**

5

SECTION D
Specialist reports

When assessing the applicant for more specialised types of fostering, consideration needs to be given as to how to evidence, in your assessment, that the applicant has the necessary experience, knowledge or skills to undertake that role. Included here are some suggestions for areas to cover when considering these more specialist areas of fostering.

Parent and child fostering

- Has the applicant got the time and space required for this kind of fostering?

- What is the applicant's understanding of what this kind of fostering involves and how realistic is this?

- What contact or discussions has the applicant had with foster carers who have experience in this area of fostering?

- What do they feel will be the rewards for them from this role?

- What is their understanding of what constitutes "good enough" parenting?

- How would they decide when to intervene in the care of a child and when to step back?

- Could the applicant provide the appropriate level of supervision to ensure that the safety of the child is paramount at all times?

- Does the applicant have the ability to make a detailed assessment of the quality of care provided by the parent?

- Does the applicant have the ability to keep sound, evidence-based records?

- Is the applicant prepared for the possibility that they might have to give evidence in court?

- Does the applicant have the potential to be able to work in partnership with a wide range of other professionals?

- Has the applicant considered the implications of potentially having another adult living in their home?

- Has the applicant considered the potential impact on other members of their household of parent and child fostering?

Permanent fostering

- What does the applicant understand by the term "permanency"?

- What is the applicant's motivation to invite a child to be a permanent member of their family?

- What is the applicant's understanding of the changes the child may experience in future years?

- How does the applicant feel about the child living with them until they leave home, in the same way their own children might (i.e. go to further education, get married), perhaps in their mid-twenties?

- What impact will this kind of fostering have on the individual members of the family?

- What age and sex of child/ren would fit in with their own family, if applicable, and why?

- What might be the potential effect on members of the extended family and friends network?

- How would permanent fostering affect the applicant financially if the fostering allowances were to cease or be reduced when the child reaches the age of 18 or 21?

- What arrangements would the applicant make if they were no longer able to care for the child for some reason in the future?

- How would the applicant feel about including the foster child (and any potential foster grandchildren) in their wills or helping to pay for events such as a wedding or helping to buy a home?

Short break fostering

- Does the applicant have the time and space in their lives to make a regular commitment to support a child by offering short breaks?

- What understanding and experience does the applicant have about children with learning and physical disabilities?

- Where there are gaps in their knowledge and experience, how will these be addressed?

- What does the applicant feel might be the purpose and benefits of short break fostering for the child and for their parent or carer?

- How can the applicant make a short break a positive experience for the child?

- What does the applicant hope to get from this kind of fostering?

- Is the applicant's home suitable for the kind of fostering proposed?

- What contact or discussions has the applicant had with foster carers who have experience in this area of fostering?

- How would short break fostering impact on other members of the family or household?

- Does the applicant have the capacity to work closely in partnership with the child's parent or carer?

Remand fostering

- Does the applicant have any relevant experience of the criminal justice system?

- What is the applicant's understanding of what remand fostering involves?

- How realistic is their understanding?

- What contact or discussions has the applicant had with foster carers who have experience in this area of fostering?

- What does the applicant hope to get from becoming a remand foster carer?

- Is the applicant aware that remand fostering can require a 24/7 level of commitment and can they evidence they can meet this?

- Is the applicant prepared for the restrictions on their own time that can be involved in supervising young people on remand?

- How would they try to ensure that any conditions of the remand were adhered to?

- Does the applicant have the flexibility to attend meetings or court at short notice?

- Does the applicant have the ability to work in partnership with a variety of different agencies and professionals such as the police, youth offending teams, legal representatives, etc?

- Has the applicant considered the implications of remand fostering for other members of the family or household?

Appendix 1: Example of an ecomap and a family tree

Note: The stronger the line linking to the applicant indicates a greater degree of support.

Mary and Peter Jones
Julie's parents
White/British
Live in same town as Julie. Daily contact by phone or visit. Currently offer practical and emotional support. Babysit Julie's children and would include any foster child. Peter enjoys DIY and making things and would share this with any foster child and would be a good role model.

David and Joanne
David is Julie's brother and Joanne his partner.
White/British
Live in Devon (200 miles from Julie) Contact by telephone monthly and see each other 2/3 times a year.
Have two children aged 18 and 16.
Offer Julie moral support but unlikely to play any major role in fostering.

JULIE (Applicant)

Winston and Claudine
Next door neighbours
African-Caribbean/British
of Catholic faith
Daily contact
Offer practical and emotional support. Would be positive support to Julie if she was caring for an African-Caribbean child. Have two children, Duane (13) and Alisha (11), who play with Julie's children and would help any foster child to settle into the neighbourhood.

Anne
Julie's best friend from school days.
Lives on same estate as Julie.
White/British.
Contact 2/3 times a week.
Offers Julie lots of moral and emotional support. Was main source of support when Julie's marriage broke up.
Anne is a single parent of two children, Anthony (9) and Suzie (7) who are of dual African-Caribbean/ White British heritage.
The two families do lots of social activities together so would play a large role in the life of any foster child.

Yoga class
Meets weekly in local community centre.
Provides Julie with valuable "me-time" as well as helping to maintain fitness and well-being.

Meera and Susan
Two friends from Julie's work.
Meera is Indian/British and Susan is White/British.
Hindu faith
Live in same town as Julie and meet up for occasional meals and nights out. Would offer Julie "time-out" from fostering.

Examplar for family tree symbols

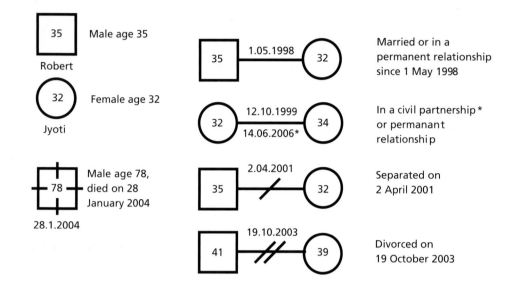

35 Robert	Male age 35
32 Jyoti	Female age 32
78 28.1.2004	Male age 78, died on 28 January 2004

35 — 1.05.1998 — 32 Married or in a permanent relationship since 1 May 1998

32 — 12.10.1999 / 14.06.2006* — 34 In a civil partnership* or permanant relationship

35 — 2.04.2001 — 32 Separated on 2 April 2001

41 — 19.10.2003 — 39 Divorced on 19 October 2003

Robert and Jyoti's family tree

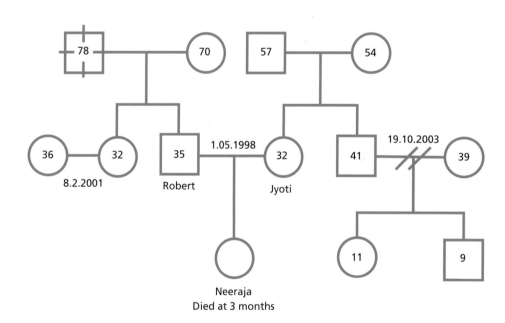

Neeraja
Died at 3 months

Appendix 2: Fostering assessment timesheet

Name of applicant/s ....

Subject covered	Completion date

About the applicants

Family background and childhood (including education)	....
Adult life (including employment and previous relationships)	....
Personality and current relationship	....
Household members (including children) and lifestyle	....
Other children (including adults) and social/support network	....

Assessment of fostering capacity

Caring for children: providing warmth, empathy and encouragement	....
Caring for children: providing structure and boundaries	....
Caring for children: providing durability, resilience and commitment	....
Working effectively with others	....
Understanding identity and diversity	....

Preparing to foster

Motivation and timing of application	....
Preparation, training and expectations	....
Anticipated impact of fostering	....
Understanding of safer caring	....
Future training and development	....

Appendix 3: Personal reference visit

Below is a suggested list of areas to cover in a personal referee interview but the assessor should also cover any specific issues that have arisen in the course of the assessment that might require verification or further exploration.

- How long have you known the applicant?

- In what capacity do you know them?

- How frequently do you have contact with them now or in the past?

- How would you describe each of the applicants (i.e. personality, temperament, etc)?

- Do you feel they have any particular qualities with regard to fostering (i.e. patience, flexibility, resilience, sense of humour, etc)?

- What do you understand their motivation for fostering to be?

- Do you have any thoughts about what age group of children or type of fostering might be appropriate for them?

- Do you consider their relationship to be a stable one?

- Do they support each other?

- Where else do the applicants get their support from?

- What support, if any, might you be able to offer them?

- If the applicants have children of their own, how would you describe them?

- Do you have any comments or observations as to the way they have brought up their own children?

- Do you have any comments or observations about how the applicants relate to other people's children?

- Are the applicants tolerant of people who are different for reasons of disability, ethnicity, religion or sexuality?

- Have you seen them under stress for any reason and, if so, how have they managed this?

- Are there any areas where you might envisage any difficulties for them in terms of fostering?

- Do you have any concerns about them abusing a child in their care?

- Do you know of any other reason why they should not foster children?

Appendix 4: Ex-partner references

Ex-partner references often raise significant feelings of anxiety for both the applicant and the assessor. Nevertheless, it is very important that these are rigorously pursued, particularly following serious case reviews such as that in Brighton and Hove (1999), when adopters gave information about a previous relationship that was not verified and, had it been so, may have prevented the death of a young child placed in their care. If applicants are aware of the reasons why these references are sought, it may help them to understand the need to pursue them.

The first issue to decide is which previous relationships are considered to be significant. This may be based on considerations such as whether children (birth or step-children) were involved in the relationship; the length and status of the relationship and how long ago it took place.

If there are felt to be valid reasons why ex-partners should not be contacted, such as in cases of domestic violence, then evidence to verify this should be sought, if possible, from official sources such as local authority, police, medical or court records. Further verification could also be sought from personal and/or family member references to support this.

If applicants are unaware of the whereabouts of their ex-partners then efforts should be made to try to locate them. The applicants themselves could try through use of social media routes. Other means could include contact through members of the ex-partners' extended family, who may not have changed address, or through mutual friends. The electoral roll could also be checked in conjunction with the online service www.192.com.

If it is decided that ex-partners should not be contacted or they cannot be located, full reasons for this or details of the efforts made should be included in the relevant part of Section A of Form F.

In those cases where ex-partners are contacted, they may be asked to provide a written reference and/or be interviewed in person. It is important for the applicant to understand that it is not expected that the reference will be an entirely positive one, although some may be. These references are to be considered in the context of other references and the assessment as a whole.

The significant areas to consider with ex-partners may include the following:

- Their view as to how and why the relationship came to an end.

- The level of contact there has been between the couple following the ending of the relationship.

- Their view with regard to the applicant's skills, capacity and suitability to care for children.

- Their views on the applicant's physical, mental and emotional health and well-being.

- Their views on the potential impact of fostering on any children of their relationship.

- Any additional comments in support of the fostering application or any other concerns they would have.

Appendix 5: Health and safety areas to consider

Below is a list of areas to consider which will help you look at issues of health and safety in the applicant's home. It is very likely that your agency will already have a checklist. Such a checklist cannot cover every potential risk so it is important to be alert for other potential dangers as you are looking around the home that are not included here, such as homes with cellars, stables, etc, and some of these issues may not be relevant for children of all ages.

Kitchen

- Is the chest freezer lockable/kept locked?
- Are kettle flexes short?
- Are knives and other sharp items safely stored?
- Are surfaces kept clean?
- Is the fridge clean and is food stored safely?
- How will safety around the cooker be ensured?
- Are cleaning materials stored safely?
- Is there a fire blanket/extinguisher?
- Is there a carbon monoxide detector?
- How is hygiene maintained in the kitchen if there are pets?

Living area

- Are rooms clean and in good decorative order?
- Is flooring clean and safe?
- Is furniture in good order?
- Does furniture conform to BSS safety standards?
- Is there sufficient heating?
- Are there any glass tables, etc, that could be a potential hazard?

- Are large areas of glass of the safety variety or are they covered with safety film?
- Is a fire guard required?
- Are 12,15 and 18 certificate DVDs/computer games stored out of view and reach?

Hallway/stairs/landing area

- Is flooring safe and in good condition?
- Are the stairs safe?
- Are banisters filled or have a maximum gap of four inches?
- Is the lighting sufficient?
- Are smoke detectors fitted and working at each level of the house?
- Are stair guards required?
- Is the area clear of clutter or any fire hazards?
- Is the key to the front door kept out of reach of young children?

Bedrooms

- Are suitable locks fitted to the windows?
- Can the windows be exited in case of fire?
- Is the room clean and light, with access to fresh air?
- Is the room in good decorative order?
- Is the flooring clean and safe?
- Is the heating sufficient for the room and fixed to the wall?
- Is there a suitable bed and bedding?
- Is the bedroom suitably furnished with storage space for the child's belongings?

Bathroom

- Is the bathroom clean and hygienic?
- Are facilities sufficient for the proposed occupants of the house?
- Is there a suitable lock on the door that could be opened in case of emergency?
- Is the light or any heater operated by a pull cord or on a switch outside the room?
- Is there a non-slip mat for the bath?
- Are shampoos and cosmetics stored out of reach of young children?
- Are razor blades and any electrical devices stored safely?

Cars/garage

- Are all vehicles taxed up to date?

- Are all vehicles covered by comprehensive insurance? On what date were the certificates seen?

- Do all vehicles have an up-to-date MOT? On what date were the certificates seen?

- Are all vehicles fitted with suitable safety restraints and child locks?

- Are the applicants aware of the regulations regarding the safe carrying of children?

- Is there a first aid kit in each vehicle?

- Are any potentially hazardous DIY fluids safely stored?

- Is all DIY equipment safely stored?

- Is there a chest freezer in the garage? Is it lockable?

- Is the garage kept locked?

Garden

- Is all gardening equipment safely locked away?

- Is the back garden securely fenced in?

- Is any play equipment safe and securely attached?

- If there is a trampoline, does it have a safety net?

- If there is a sandpit, is it clean and hygienic?

- Are any garden ponds safely covered or securely fenced in?

- Are there ponds or hazards in neighbouring gardens that might pose a risk?

- Is any greenhouse fitted with safety glass and kept locked?

- Is the garden kept clear of pet waste?

- If there is a swimming pool or hot tub, is it kept safely covered and maintained?

General

- Is alcohol stored safely and out of reach?

- Are cigarettes, including e-cigarettes, lighters and matches stored safely and out of reach?

- Are gas appliances and boiler serviced annually? On what date were the safety certificates seen?

- Is there a fire escape plan?

- Are medicines stored safely and securely?

- Is there a first aid box with suitable and in-date contents?

- Do any toys in the home appear clean and safe and comply with safety standards?

- If the applicant has guns in the house, are they securely stored and does the applicant have a licence that has been checked?

- Do any pets appear safe, friendly and hygienically cared for?

- Have individual assessments been undertaken on each dog in the home?

- Is there adequate buildings and contents insurance? On what date were the certificates seen?

- Where the applicant lives on a farm, there should be particular attention paid to safety in relation to machinery, outbuildings, accessibility to farm land and contact with farm animals.

Appendix 6: Safer caring

Below are some issues to consider with regards to safer caring. It is likely that your agency has a safer caring policy that can be shared with the applicant.

- Maintaining privacy in the home
- Supervising children within the home (to include use of computers and mobile phones)
- Monitoring children outside the home
- Dressing appropriately
- Transporting children
- Washing and bathtime routines
- Bedtime routines
- First aid/understanding of HIV and other blood-borne infections
- Family fire safety plan
- Physical contact
- Showing affection
- Use of restraint
- Taking photographs and making videos
- Keeping records
- Ensuring safety of friends and family network

Appendix 7: References and further reading

Adams P and Dibben E (2011) *Parent and Child Fostering*, London: BAAF

Adams P (2015) *Dogs and Pets in Fostering and Adoption*, London: BAAF

BAAF (2011) *Using the Internet in Adoption and Fostering Assessments*, London: BAAF

Beesley P (2015) *Making Good Assessments*, London: CoramBAAF

Bilfuco A (2012) *Introduction to the Attachment Style Interview*, available at: www.attachmentstyleinterview.com

Chapman R, *Welcome to our Family: The Board Game of Fostering*, available from CoramBAAF

CoramBAAF Guidance Notes on Prospective Carers Report, available from CoramBAAF, attached to Form F

CoramBAAF (2015) *Undertaking Overseas Checks in Fostering and Adoption Assessments*, London: CoramBAAF

Cosis Brown H (2016) *Foster Carer Reviews*, London: CoramBAAF (For useful summary of Serious Case Reviews)

Cosis Brown H, Sebba J and Lake N (2015) *The Recruitment, Assessment, Support and Supervision of Lesbian, Gay and Transgender Foster Carers: An international review*, Oxford: Rees Centre, University of Oxford, available at: http://reescentre.education.ox.ac.uk/research/publications/lgbtfostercarers-review/

Cousins J (2010) *Pushing the Boundaries of Assessment*, London: BAAF

De Jong A and Donnelly S (2015) *Recruiting, Assessing and Supporting Lesbian and Gay Adopters*, London: BAAF

Department for Education (2013) *Assessment and Approval of Foster Carers. Amendments to the Children Act 1989. Guidance and Regulations – Volume 4*, London: Department for Education

Quinton D, Rushton A, Dance C and Mayes D (1998) *Joining New Families:* A study of adoption and fostering in middle childhood, Chichester: Wiley

Schofield G and Beek M (2014) *The Secure Base Model*, London: BAAF. Also see: www.uea.ac.uk/providingsecurebase/home: click on 'Resources' for a one-hour lecture by Gillian Schofield giving an introduction to the Secure Base Model. An assessment of prospective foster carers and adopters using the model can also be printed off from this website.

Sinclair I, Wilson K and Gibbs I (2004) *Foster Placements: Why they succeed and why they fail*, London: Jessica Kingsley Publishers

Slade J (2012) *Safer Caring: A new approach*, London: Fostering Network

Smith F and Brann C (2016) *Fostering Now: Law, regulations, guidance and standards*, London: CoramBAAF

Helpful titles for applicants

Bond H (ed) (2005) *If You Don't Stick With Me, Who Will? The challenges and rewards of foster care*, London: BAAF

Camis J (2003) *We Are Fostering: A workbook for birth children*, London: BAAF

Glass C (2007) *Damaged*, and other titles by Cathy Glass

Miles L (2010) *Holding On and Hanging In*, London: BAAF

Titles published by BAAF and CoramBAAF are available through CoramBAAF. Visit www.corambaaf.org.uk/bookshop for more information or to order, or contact 020 7520 7517.